DON'T SETTLE FOR THE

Sex of It!

A SELF-LOVE GUIDE
to Sexual Self-Respect

For Women & Those Who Love Them

RAQUEL SYMONE

Table of Contents

I want to extend my deepest gratitude to you for choosing to purchase and read, *"Don't Settle for the 'Sex' of It! A Guide to Sexual Self-Respect (For Women and Those Who Love Them)"*. Your decision to invest your time and energy into this book means the world to me, and I am truly honored to be a part of your journey toward self-discovery and empowerment.

This book was written with love, care, and a profound respect for the strength it takes to stand firm in your values, especially in a world that often encourages us to compromise. By choosing to preserve your sexual and emotional energy, you are not only honoring yourself but also setting a powerful example for others. You recognize the immense worth of your body, your heart, and your spirit, and you have made the courageous decision to save these gifts for the partner who is worthy of your love and commitment. Congratulations! I celebrate your resolve to wait for the one who will choose you as his wife, who will cherish you for the incredible woman you are, and who will honor the sacred bond that you both share.

This is not just a journey of waiting—it's a journey of self-respect, self-love, and deep emotional fulfillment. Thank you for allowing me to walk alongside you on this path. I hope the words in this book inspire, encourage, and uplift you as you continue to hold your standards high and live a life that reflects the beautiful, strong, and valuable person you are.

With heartfelt appreciation and warmest regards,

Raquel Symone

THIS PAGE LEFT
BLANK INTENTIONALLY

A Personal Note of Gratitude

To the village of people who have shaped and supported me—including my family, friends, colleagues, and all those I've had the privilege to serve—thank you for remaining loyal in your love and inspiration.

To those past relationships that taught me to grow and gave me the space to evolve, I'm grateful for the lessons embedded in those chapters.

My deepest appreciation goes to my Veteran community for ensuring that mental health care has been not only accessible but exceptional.

To my therapists, whole health coaches, and every caregiver along the way, thank you for guiding me toward healing and wholeness. Your influence has been a profound part of this journey. Together, we are building a movement—one that uplifts and transforms, helping to save the souls of those seeking redemption and a better path forward. Your love and guidance have been the foundation of this calling.

To my Army Veteran sister, Lori Wilcox—thank you for showing me the path to writing a book, for loving me like only a true sister could, and for being a shining example of feminine grace and class. Though you are no longer with us, your legacy lives on, and you will never be forgotten.

THIS PAGE LEFT
BLANK INTENTIONALLY

A Note to the *Honorable* Men Who *Love Women*

To the men who cherish and honor the women in their lives, this book is not only a guide for women, but also a tribute to you. While the content within these pages is focused on empowering women to strengthen their self-love and embrace their true worth, it is equally about becoming the kind of woman who is worthy of the love and respect that only a good man can provide.

We recognize and honor the men who patiently respect our decision to wait for marriage, understanding that this choice is not just about us—it's about building a foundation of trust, honesty respect, and loyalty that honors an emotional connection worthy of your last name. Your patience, commitment to upholding high standards, and your willingness to seek out a woman who you can truly provide for and lead are qualities that deserve our deepest admiration.

This book is written with you in mind, as much as it is for us. It is a journey towards becoming the woman who will stand by your side, not just as a partner, but as the chosen one—the woman you can proudly cherish as a wife.

We honor you for recognizing that true femininity is not just about beauty, but about a deep inner strength, kindness, and compassion.

We respect you for seeking a woman who embodies these qualities, and for being the kind of man who values and nurtures them.

As you read this book, know that we appreciate you, we see you, and we are grateful for your role in our lives. Your standards inspire us to be better, to rise to the occasion, and to prepare ourselves to be the woman you can trust, love, and build a life with. Thank you for being the men who see beyond the surface and for choosing to walk alongside us on this journey for lifelong partnership.

My Continuous Gratitude

First and foremost, I offer my deepest gratitude to my gracious Lord and Savior, the Almighty Creator of my life. Thank you for the endless blessings, inspiration, and protection You have provided on my journey. I embrace this mission to uplift and help others, especially women, with full faith in Your plan. And I thank You in advance for the delivery of my wonderful king, a partner who will walk with me in purpose and love.

To my beautiful children, my heart and soul: Your love and support are unmatched. All that I do, every step I take, is for you and our future generations, so that you may have brighter opportunities and a life filled with joy. I hope I have been a source of inspiration to you as you continue to reach for your own dreams. Watching you grow into the remarkable individuals you are today fills me with pride. Your accomplishments reflect your strength, determination, and the love we share. Keep shining, because you are my greatest legacy.

To my sweet inner princess: I see you, and I honor you. You have always been, and always will be, worthy of love, protection, and happiness. Together, we are embracing the joy, love, and peace that was meant for us all along. Your beauty, strength, and worth radiate from within, and I will continue to nurture and protect you as we grow. You are a precious gem, deserving of the love that is waiting for you, and never forget—you are enough, just as you are.

To my alter ego, DJ Rock Hell: You are *my* rock and a guiding light in the darkest times. Through your love of life and music, you've blessed not just me but everyone we've encountered with infectious joy. Let's keep spinning those records and lighting up every room we walk into—because with you, the music never stops, and neither does the magic.

To my supportive and loving friends, both here and those who are no longer with us: Your presence in my life has been a gift beyond measure. For those who have passed on, your spirits remain with me, and the lessons, laughter, and love we shared will stay with me forever. You left an imprint on my heart that continues to guide me.

To my friends who walk this journey with me today, your unwavering support lifts me higher every day. I am so thankful for your friendship, loyalty, and love.

To my veteran community: I am beyond proud to stand beside such an elite group of men and women, a family bonded by service, sacrifice, and the will to persevere. Together, we hold each other accountable, share in each other's triumphs, and lift one another up when life weighs us down. The work we do is more than service—it is a labor of love, and I am honored to be in the company of such brave souls who embody resilience and unity.

To all my past intimate relationships: Thank you for the love, lessons, and growth you poured into my life. Though our paths separated, each relationship carried profound purpose and meaning. We crossed paths when we were meant to, and from each of you, I have taken invaluable lessons that shaped the woman I am today. Sometimes, good people meet at the wrong time, but the impact remains. I hold no regrets—only gratitude for the love we shared and the ways it has helped me evolve.

To my mental health care providers: Thank you for your attention to detail, your patience, and your compassion. You created a safe space for me to express every emotion without judgment, allowing me to heal and grow. Your guidance has been instrumental in my journey of self-discovery and emotional well-being.

To my business partners and collaborators: Your belief in this project, your dedication, and your hard work made the creation of this book possible. Thank you for walking beside me, for sharing your talents, and for helping me bring this vision to life.

To the people I may not have specifically named: Please know that you are remembered and appreciated. Your influence and support have been part of the foundation that brought me here today. For every conversation, word of encouragement, and act of kindness, I thank you from the depths of my heart.

How to Use This Guide

In a world where too often we give away our bodies without considering the emotional cost, many of us are left scarred with the pain and disappointment of settling. Here is where you pull them big girl panties right back up and regain your dignity and self-respect with accountability. We've all made mistakes—we've slept with, had children with, and married men who didn't deserve us. Take a long deep breath sis, you will be okay. The pages ahead are your sanctuary, a place where you can begin to forgive yourself for the poor choices of the past and learn to recognize that good men will never judge you for where you've been.

NOTE: This book is not a manual on 'finding a man'; rather, it's a transformative journey towards changing your behaviors and perspectives. By embracing the principles within these pages, you'll learn to attract the kind of man who is not only captivated by your presence, but is also worthy of your body and a lifelong commitment.

This book is about shedding the shame that has weighed you down and rebuilding yourself from the inside out. It's about nurturing your mind, body, and soul so that you can be ready to attract and be noticed by the right kind of man—the man who values you for who you are and who you've become. Use this guide as a tool to cleanse yourself of harmful thoughts, to reclaim your self-worth, and to strengthen the positive femininity within you that naturally repels toxic, no-good men.

Put God First & Good Men Will Follow

With so many distractions and noise around us, it's easy to lose sight of what truly matters. We often find ourselves chasing after relationships, hoping to find love and fulfillment in another person. But have you ever stopped to consider that the greatest relationship you could ever cultivate is the one you have with God?

When you allow God into your life first, you open yourself to His guidance, wisdom, and love. You start to see yourself through His eyes—valued, cherished, and worthy of the best. This foundation in faith is not just about finding solace or comfort; it's about aligning your life with His purpose and plans for you. By putting God at the center, you create space for Him to work in your life, including in your relationships.

A man of God is someone who seeks the same divine guidance in his life. He is drawn to the light that shines within you when you are rooted in your faith. By allowing God to lead your steps, you naturally attract someone who is also walking in faith, and who understands the importance of building a relationship on the principles of love, respect, and commitment as outlined in God's Word.

How many times will you meet someone
you thought was *"the one,"*
only to discover they're far from it?

Self-love is designed to enlighten, but it may also stir up reflections on past decisions and behaviors. Take a breath, beautiful—the goal isn't to shame or judge, but to empower you. If you're ready to clean up your emotional health and reclaim your sexual power, it starts with an honest look at your past relationships and the choices you've made. This journey requires intention and a commitment to changing what no longer serves you. Let's begin by identifying where you currently stand—whether single and exploring, engaged, or somewhere in between—so we can move forward with clarity and purpose.

Single & Promiscuous

Now, this may be challenging for those with a vibrant sexual appetite, but the choice is yours. And that's the point: ***Choose You First!*** Often, we engage in premarital sex to appease someone else, out of fear of losing them or giving in to pressure, but we don't have to do this.

After reading this book and reflecting on the affirmations and exercises, I hope you'll come to understand your worth and realize there's a world of **great** men waiting to meet a woman who has preserved her body specifically for him. While this doesn't guarantee a forever marriage, it does encourage a deeper connection and increases the chances of a lifelong commitment based on more than just sex.

So, before you let your hormones and passion take the lead, pause. Take a deep breath, gather your thoughts, and refocus on self-love.

Set your boundaries with confidence, embrace your intentions with clarity, and trust that as you focus on God, He will guide your journey. Rest in your feminine energy, knowing that the ultimate relationship is with God, and as you work on yourself, the right man will find you in His perfect timing. If you are already in a **sexual relationship**, consider this:

Situationships

If you find yourself in a situationship (a sexual relationship that is undefined and non committal, often one-sided) this workbook is here to guide you toward realizing the value you deserve. Understand that it's never too late to set boundaries and reclaim your worth. Start by working on your femininity, becoming more in tune with your aura, and slowly pulling away from the sexual and wifely duties that aren't being reciprocated with the commitment you deserve. Move in silence—protect your peace and allow this book to help you transition to a place of self-respect, where you demand more for yourself without fear of losing someone who was never truly yours to begin with. You are worthy of a love that honors and uplifts you, not one that uses you and leaves you drained.

Exclusive Sexual Relationship, but Not Married

If you believe you are in a healthy relationship and a piece of paper is not necessary, congratulations sis, we are proud of you! This book is for those who aren't so fortunate and are tapped out emotionally from giving away their bodies at the expense of their sexual self-respect.

When God is first in your life, you are less likely to settle for anything less than His best. You develop a sense of discernment that helps you recognize when a relationship is not aligned with His will. You learn to trust in His timing, knowing that He is preparing both you and your future partner for a union that reflects His love.

Allowing God to lead also means surrendering your worries, fears, and desires to Him. It means trusting that He knows the desires of your heart and that He is more than capable of bringing the right person into your life. A man of God will recognize your commitment to faith, and he will be drawn to it. He will value your dedication to living a life that honors God, and together you will build a relationship that is not just grounded in love for each other, but also in love for the One who brought you together.

So, let God be first in your life. Seek Him, trust Him, and allow His presence to guide your every decision. As you deepen your relationship with Him, you will find that He is already orchestrating the meeting of two hearts that are destined to be one under His divine care. A man of God will see the beauty of your faith, and he will be honored to walk alongside you on this journey of life and love.

Remember, trusting yourself is the first step to true peace of mind. Saving your body, protecting your emotional well-being, and refusing to give in to premarital sex are acts of self-love and protection. These actions will shield you from the wrong kind of men and pave the way for the right one to come into your life.

Engaged Couples

For those who counter the arguments presented by saying, "But we're going to get married anyway." "We're in love and have a spiritual commitment." "What difference does it make if we become *'one flesh'* right now or wait until after the wedding?"

This guide serves as a subtle cautionary sign: YOU HAVE NOT OFFICIALLY COMMITTED, even if you're engaged. In our culture, engagement doesn't amount to that kind of promise. It's not the sort of commitment that requires you to step over a line you can't re-cross without some serious social and legal consequences. The real promise will be given when you stand before God in the assembly of witnesses and solemnly pledge yourselves to one another *"til death do you part."* Until those vows are said, it's still fairly easy to bail out.

This leads to an important point. It's not uncommon for weddings to be canceled a week or even moments before the event. Such things do happen. When they do, couples who have already had sexual intercourse end up carrying more emotional and psychological baggage than those who have made the decision to wait before having sex.

As you work through this guide, consider the investment of your emotions, time, and sexual health.

How many more fleeting encounters will you
endure just to satisfy a moment of lust,
only to feel empty or at a loss afterward?

Submissively Celibate

Positive femininity is your super power—it's what will set you apart and draw in the man who sees your worth, cherishes your essence, and is ready to build a life with you that's rooted in mutual respect and deep, lasting love.

As you turn these pages, know that you're taking the first steps towards a brighter, healthier, and more fulfilling future. Trust the process, honor your journey, and embrace the incredible woman you are becoming. The right man will notice, and he will cherish every bit of the work you've done to become the woman you were always meant to be.

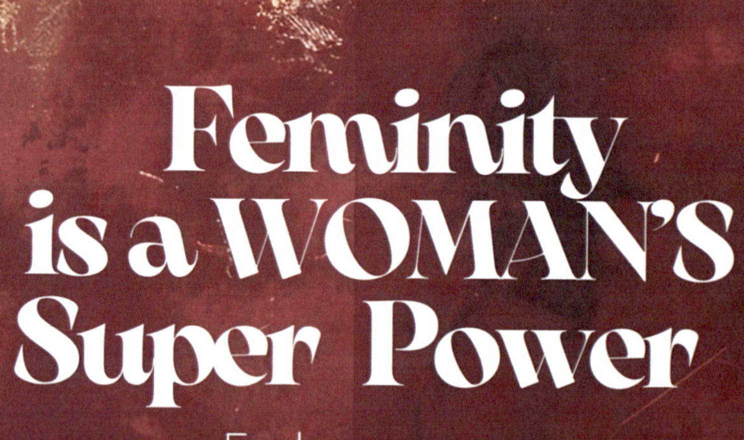
Feminity
is a WOMAN'S
Super Power
Embrace yours.

Embrace Your Femininity

Femininity is often misrepresented as merely a collection of external attributes—clothing, hair, makeup, and accessories. While these are certainly expressions of femininity, the true essence of a woman's feminine nature lies far deeper. It's in her aura, the way she moves through the world with grace and kindness, and how she interacts with others with a gentle and compassionate heart.

A *truly feminine woman* possesses a softness that isn't about weakness, but about strength in vulnerability.

Her kindness is not merely an action but a reflection of her inner peace and self-love. This kind of femininity is magnetic—it's sought after without a word being spoken. When she does speak, her voice is soft, not because she is silenced, but because she understands the power of gentle words and the influence they carry.

Femininity is also about balance. It's about being a helpmate who is fit, not just physically, but emotionally and spiritually. It's about embracing positive masculinity, supporting and nurturing it, while never compromising on self-respect or personal boundaries. The essence of femininity is a powerful force that enhances and complements masculinity, creating harmony and strength in relationships.

Femininity is not about adhering to societal expectations or fitting into a mold. It's about embracing the qualities that make you uniquely you and allowing them to flourish. As you strengthen your femininity, you'll find that it becomes a source of power, attracting positive energy and creating harmony in all areas of your life.

Ways to *Strengthen* and *Embrace* Your Femininity

Cultivate Inner Peace

True femininity shines when a woman is at peace with herself. While empathy is a strength, remember that you are not obligated to absorb the drama of others. Offer support without sacrificing your own peace, and never try to fix someone else at the expense of your well-being. Protect your energy, and let your inner harmony be your guiding force.

Speak Softly & Kindly

Learn the art of being assertive with class. Stand firm in your truth while maintaining grace, even in challenging situations. Use your voice to uplift, encourage, and soothe. Practice speaking in a calm, gentle tone that reflects your inner confidence and compassion. In moments of anger, avoid swearing or shouting, as these only escalate the situation. Instead, embrace the strength of composure, knowing that real power comes from staying centered.

Nurture Your Body & Health

Femininity flourishes in a healthy body. Prioritize fitness, eat nourishing foods, and engage in activities that keep you strong and vibrant. Your body is a temple; treat it with the respect it deserves. No smoking of any kind and eliminate or seriously limit alcohol.

Be Compassionate & Kind

Kindness is the essence of femininity. Offer a helping hand, volunteer for charity, and engage in acts of service. When you give to others, you also give to yourself, enriching your spirit and deepening your feminine nature.

Embrace Your Role As A Helpmate

Support and nurture the positive masculinity in your life. This doesn't mean submission in the traditional sense, but rather a harmonious partnership where both individuals uplift and strengthen each other.

Visit www.raquelsymone.com to learn more about the Art of Submission workshops.

Practice Self-Care & Pampering

Femininity is about enjoying the beauty of life. Pamper yourself with rituals that make you feel beautiful inside and out—whether it's a relaxing bath, a new outfit, or simply taking time to do something you love.

Always remain polished from top to bottom.

Engage In Creative Expression

Whether it's through art, writing, dance, or any other form of creativity, *expressing yourself artistically* can deepen your connection to your feminine energy.

Be Present & Mindful

Femininity flourishes when you are fully engaged with life as it unfolds. Practice being truly present in your daily activities- whether you're working, spending time with loved ones, or even enjoying a quiet moment for yourself. Resist the urge to multitask or become distracted by worries. Instead, focus on the here and now, offering your full attention to the moment at hand. This will not only strengthen your connections with others, but also allow you to experience life more deeply and authentically.

Establish & Set Your Boundaries

Good men LOVE women who prioritize self-respect. Say NO and mean it! Never be afraid to walk away from people or relationships that do not align with your boundaries.

INSPIRATION
KEEP pushing BOUNDARIES AND never STOP EVOLVING.

Honoring
Your Boundaries...
Is Your Armor.

No More Using Your *'Sweet P'* Just for the Sex of It

Don't Settle for the 'Sex' of It, My Beauty Warriors

In choosing to honor yourself, you are protecting more than just your body—you are safeguarding your emotional and sexual well-being. Whether you wait until marriage or simply choose to respect your worth along the way, you are preserving the sanctity of your soul and ensuring that your heart is honored in the way it deserves. Your boundaries are a reflection of the love and value you hold for yourself, and they set the standard for how others will treat you.

When you embrace your self-worth and commit to protecting your emotional health, you create the foundation for a future where you are cherished and respected, both by yourself and by the healthy partner who recognizes your value. This isn't just about waiting for your wedding night —it's about honoring the journey to becoming a whole, empowered woman who is worthy of the kind of love that uplifts and respects her.

No more using your body just for the *'sex'* of it. Hold fast to your boundaries, stand firm in your worth, and remember, the one who recognizes and honors your value is worth the wait, whether that comes before or after marriage.

Setting Boundaries with Strength & Clarity

When someone challenges your boundaries, use these statements to clearly express your needs, while maintaining respect for both yourself and the relationship. These responses allow you to protect your well-being and encourage healthier, more respectful interactions:

1. My "no" is not negotiable.
2. The things I allowed in the past no longer work for me.
3. It's understood if you don't like what I'm saying, but I need you to respect it.
4. I mentioned this solution because I do want to maintain the relationship.
5. It's apparent we think differently about this, but I will not debate about what feels healthy for me.
6. I appreciate your input, but this is something I've already decided is non-negotiable for me.
7. I've been clear about what I need, and I won't compromise on it.
8. Respecting my boundaries is essential for our relationship to thrive.
9. I understand your perspective, but this is what I need to feel safe.
10. I value our relationship, but I also need to value myself.
11. I hear you, but I'm comfortable with this, and I need you to understand where I'm coming from.
12. My boundary isn't about controlling you, it's about protecting me.
13. I can't continue this conversation if my boundaries aren't respected.
14. My well-being is a non-negotiable.
15. I've already expressed how I feel about this, and I'm asking that you respect my decision.

Your **body** is not a
bargaining chip
and ***your soul*** is not
for sale!

RAQUEL SYMONE

Protect
Your
Pearls!

The world is *your oyster.*
Cherish your pearls.

"Do not give dogs what is holy; do not throw your pearls before swine. If you do, they may trample them under their feet, and then turn and tear you to pieces."
- Matthew 7:6

This passage from the Bible holds a profound lesson that resonates deeply with me. It speaks to the importance of guarding what is sacred and precious—specifically, the sanctity of your body and your self-worth.

Imagine your body, your essence, as a strand of the most exquisite pearls. These pearls represent your purity, your values, your love, and everything that makes you uniquely you. They are a symbol of your inner beauty, grace, and the dignity that you carry as a woman. Pearls are delicate, timeless, and require careful handling to maintain their luster. Similarly, your body and spirit deserve to be cherished and protected, not given away carelessly to those who cannot appreciate their worth.

This scripture is a powerful reminder: Do not give what is sacred—your "pearls"—to those who do not deserve them. Low-functioning men, or individuals who vibrate at a low frequency, will never treasure or honor the gift of your love and your body.

Just like swine that cannot appreciate the value of pearls, they may trample on what you offer, leaving you feeling used, disrespected, and heartbroken. These are the ones who, after taking what they want, may turn around and hurt you—whether through physical harm, emotional abuse, or by tarnishing your reputation.

Take heed to this wisdom not only when choosing a potential mate, but in all your interactions. Recognize the value of your pearls and do not cast them before those who cannot see their worth. Instead, protect them, polish them, and wear them proudly as a testament to the elegance, class, and dignity that define you.

In doing so, you'll find that those who truly deserve your pearls—those who are capable of appreciating and treasuring them—will see your sparkle from afar. They will approach you with the respect and admiration you deserve, ready to honor and cherish the gift that you are.

As you navigate your journey, remember this: You are a pearl, a precious gem that deserves to be valued and protected. Guard your pearls with care, and only offer them to someone who sees you for the priceless treasure you truly are.

The world is your oyster, and within that oyster lies the power to create something beautiful, rare, and valuable. Like the pearls that take time to form, your self-worth and the love you have for yourself must be cultivated with care. When you present yourself with class and elegance, you set a standard for how others will treat you. This begins with how you see yourself and the choices you make in whom you allow into your life.

Your "Sweet P"

Let's Talk About **Sex** &
Honoring Your **True Value**

No more sugar coating, let's talk about sex, sis! It's not just a physical act—it's an exchange of energy, emotions, and intimacy. Every time you share your body, you're sharing a part of yourself, especially your emotional and spiritual self. And here's the truth: sex has the power to create an illusion of closeness. It can make us feel connected when in reality, there's no real foundation beneath it. Without the solid ground of genuine emotional intimacy, what's left after the act? Often, it's an emptiness, a void we didn't expect.

The more casual encounters we allow, the more fragmented our emotional energy becomes. Our **"sweet P"** is precious, but sometimes we hand it over like a prize for empty promises, shallow compliments, and manipulative sweet talk. How often have you given your time, energy, and your most sacred part to someone who didn't deserve it, simply because they said the right words at the right time? We've all been there, hoping that maybe this time he'll see our worth, or maybe this time the promises will be real. But let's be real, they rarely are.

Your vagina—your *"sweet P"*—isn't just a physical part of you. It's your pearl, a gift from God.

It's not to be cast before swine, and it certainly isn't meant for men who bring nothing but empty promises and low-vibrating energy into your life. It's time to treat your body, especially your **"sweet P,"** like the treasure it is.

This isn't about depriving yourself—it's about honoring YOU. Your pearl is sacred, and everybody is not worthy of it. You have the responsibility to guard, protect, and value your pearl, just as God intended.

So, let's stop settling. Let's stop rewarding manipulation, shallow flattery, and hollow gestures with something as precious as our **"sweet P."** Let's start respecting ourselves enough to say, "I am worthy of more." And trust me, sis, when you honor your pearl, the right man—one who values **ALL** of you—will come along. Because men who are swine? They can't even recognize a pearl when they see one.

There comes a moment when you have to ask yourself: *"What am I really giving away?"* Sex, at its core, is an intimate exchange, but when you keep handing over pieces of your body without recognizing its value, you're not just giving away sex—you're giving away parts of your soul.

It's time for accountability. You owe it to yourself to ask: *"Why have I allowed this? Why have I settled for less than what I truly deserve?"* It's easy to blame the past—absent fathers, childhood traumas, neglect—but the truth is, there comes a point where you have to stop looking back for answers and start looking in the mirror. No more hiding behind the pain that shaped you. It's time to take responsibility for the woman you are now and the choices you continue to make.

Are you truly honoring yourself when you give your body to a man you barely know, hoping he'll fill the void within you? Is that fleeting connection enough to soothe the loneliness, or is it a temporary escape from the real work—healing? This isn't about shaming you; it's about waking you up. Your body is not a bargaining chip for love or validation. It's a temple, and it deserves reverence.

Ask yourself honestly: "Why do I keep repeating these patterns?" Is it the fear of being alone?

Or is it the fear of being fully seen and loved by a good man, one who respects you and your boundaries? Sometimes it's easier to settle for temporary thrills than to face the discomfort of true intimacy and being vulnerable in the presence of real love.

But here's the tough truth: you can't blame your past forever. You can't continue to carry the weight of your childhood traumas as an excuse for why you're giving pieces of yourself away. At some point, you have to own your decisions and the soul ties you've created. You have to want more for yourself. You have to believe that you are worthy of more.

Cutting those ties isn't easy. It requires you to dig deep, to confront your fears, and to let go of the toxic belief that sex equals love. It doesn't. And deep down, you know that. The men who come and go don't heal your wounds—they only deepen them. It's time to stop using sex as a substitute for the emotional work you need to do.

Real love, the kind you're longing for, starts with you. It starts with honoring yourself enough to say "no" when your soul is whispering that this isn't what you need. It starts with respecting your body as something sacred, not as a tool for temporary validation. You don't need to settle for less just to feel wanted in the moment. You're worthy of so much more than that.

Take accountability for the choices you've made, but don't dwell in shame. Recognize them as lessons learned and move forward with intention. The next time you think about giving yourself away, pause. Ask yourself: *Am I honoring the woman I'm becoming, or am I settling for the woman I've outgrown?*

The Real Toll
On Your Soul

LET'S TALK ABOUT IT

These pages are a safe space for you, sis, because we're about to dive deep into some real talk—no judgment, just love and truth.

Ladies, let's talk about your Sweet 'P.' Yep, your precious "pearl" deserves the same love and care you'd give a luxury car or your favorite pair of shoes—because honey child, if something's off down there, it's not something you can ignore! If you're noticing unpleasant smells or extra discharge, trust me, everyone else can too. Don't wait------ get your "p" health in check. Think of it as giving your Sweet 'P' a tune-up. And while we're on the topic, let's have a real chat: whether you use condoms or not, having multiple partners can cause a whole lot of funk besides bacterial vaginosis. Much worse is a soul tie. I mean, your Sweet 'P' is like a VIP section—letting too many in is bound to cause chaos! So, take this time of abstinence to consult professionals, figure out what foods or habits might be throwing things off, and get your Sweet 'P' in peak condition. When your soulmate arrives, you'll be more than ready to *drop it low and spread it wide*, inviting your king to enjoy the fresh *'whip'* you've kept polished just for him!

It's completely understandable if the rush of this fast-paced world makes you feel like you need to move at lightning speed when it comes to relationships. We're bombarded with instant gratification and the constant pressure to keep up with the latest trends. This "microwave effect" has seeped into how we approach relationships, where the focus is on quick, easy connections rather than deep, meaningful ones.

Take a moment to reflect on why you might be giving away your body so easily.

Are you truly connecting with the person you're with, or are you seeking validation, comfort, or a fleeting sense of intimacy?

It's important to ask yourself these questions because, in many cases, the answers reveal a deeper need for something that a physical connection alone cannot satisfy.

We live in an era where communication has become almost entirely digital. Texting, phone calls, and online dating have replaced face-to-face conversations, creating a false sense of closeness. It's easy to mistake constant messaging for genuine connection, but the truth is these interactions often lack depth and substance. They may satisfy a temporary craving for attention, but they rarely build the emotional foundation needed for a lasting relationship.

When you hand out your body like free samples to every person who catches your eye, you're not just giving away a piece of yourself—you're inviting a whirlwind of emotional, mental, and physical chaos. That quick fling might seem fun in the moment, but it could leave you with more than you bargained for: a smelly vagina, an unwanted pregnancy, an STD, and a soul tie that's harder to shake than last year's bad decision. You're left tangled in a sticky web of emotions, broken, and drained—leaving nothing but fragments for your future husband. So, take care of your *Sweet 'P'* and your soul. Trust me, it's worth saving the best of yourself for the one who's willing to invest in all of you.

The ease of modern communication has made it simple to fall into patterns of shallow relationships that are more about convenience than real connection.

- Let's ditch the ***'friends with benefits'*** game and ask: what benefit are you really getting? Isn't it time to hold out for someone who values your mind, spirit, and heart—not just your body?

- Why stay stuck in a **'situationship'** where you're the emotional support and they barely show up for you? You deserve a partner who's all in, not someone who just takes without giving back.

Forming soul ties prematurely can weigh heavily on your spirit, leaving you feeling drained, confused, and disconnected from your true self. The cost of bonding with someone who isn't ready to truly invest in your soul is far greater than the fleeting moments of pleasure. The key to a fulfilling relationship lies in building a connection that goes beyond the superficial. It's about finding someone who's willing to invest time and effort to understand the depths of who you are—not just someone who's after what's easily within reach.

Ask yourself:

- Are you engaging in these fast-paced, superficial relationships out of fear, loneliness, or the desire to fit in.

- Are you giving your body away in hopes of securing a relationship that, deep down, you know isn't right for you?

If so, it's time to take a step back and focus on nurturing relationships that are built on trust, respect, and genuine affection.

Remember, your body is precious. It deserves to be cherished by someone who values you for all that you are, not just for your **sweet "P"**. By taking the time to connect with someone on a deeper level before becoming physically involved, you're setting the stage for a relationship that has the potential to be truly fulfilling.

Everything around you might be speeding up, but you have the power to set your own pace sis. Take the time to build connections that matter, to find someone who appreciates the real you, and to ensure that your body, mind, and soul are respected in every relationship you enter. Your worth is not determined by how quickly you give yourself away, but by how deeply you value yourself and the relationships you choose to nurture.

I encourage you to continue to be honest by asking yourself some tough questions.

Are you truly being courted or do you find yourself caught up in endless cycles of texting and lengthy phone conversations that create the illusion of a deep connection? It's easy to feel like you know someone when words flow freely behind screens or across phone lines, but it's important to step back and assess the reality of your interactions.

Really reflect and ask yourself the following questions to better understand the nature of your connections:

- Am I engaging in casual sex as a quick way to connect? Consider if physical intimacy is acting as a shortcut to what you hope will be a deeper bond.

- Am I giving in to premarital sex out of fear of losing this person? Reflect on whether the fear of their departure is driving you to compromise your boundaries.

- Is sex the primary foundation of our connection? Evaluate if your relationship has depth beyond physical encounters.

- Do I often feel empty and disconnected after our encounters? Acknowledge your feelings post-interaction to determine if your emotional needs are truly being met.

- Is this person actively contributing to my life, such as taking me on meaningful dates, or do I feel consistently unfulfilled? Assess how much this person invests in you beyond the bedroom.

Understanding the answers to these questions can guide you in respecting your sexual boundaries and ensure you are not settling for less than you deserve. Remember, good men exist—men who will honor your decision to wait, appreciate your personality, and invest in a relationship that fulfills you emotionally and spiritually. They are the ones who will want to court you properly, showing that they value not just a part of you, but all of you.

In the upcoming sections, we'll celebrate the behaviors of good men who know how to truly respect and treat a woman, emphasizing that respecting yourself attracts the kind of partner who will respect you too, but first lets address something really important that may be blocking your blessing.

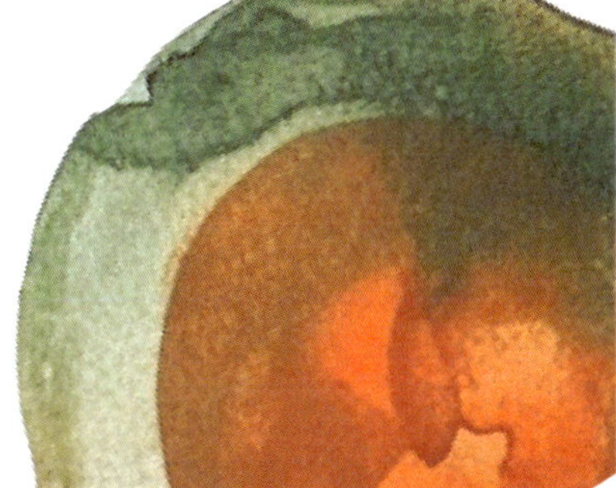

Letting Go of Shame

Some of you reading this may be living with the weight of shame over poor decisions you've made in the past. Perhaps you dated several men, slept with each of them, and had a few *"drive-bys"* in between. Maybe you even had children with some of them. You might have been performing wifely duties—cooking, cleaning, and even offering intimacy on demand—with the promise that if you kept it up, he would marry you. You believed that your relationships, situationships, or one-night stands—whatever you label them—would lead to the promise of marriage. But that never happened, and now you're struggling as a single mom, burdened by soul ties.

Here's the truth: none of that matters if you're willing to do the work on yourself. You can level up your mind, clean up your life as it stands, and prepare for a good man. He is out there—willing, able, and ready to step in and show you the actions of a KING.

Listen, only you know your body count, and that's where it should stay. A good man, a godly man, doesn't concern himself with your past. He knows who he is and is ready to go to W.A.R. (Willing, Able, Ready) for the right woman. He's **willing** to accept your children and release you from survival mode into a loving, stable environment where you **all** can thrive.

He is **able** to provide for you mentally and financially, allowing you to rest in your femininity and be his peace; and he is **ready** to protect you and his family at all costs so that you never have to feel the effects of your past traumas or poor decisions again.

But understand, this man is a high-functioning, healed, and conscious individual. To attract and keep him, you must be the same. Learn from your mistakes and become the peace that he seeks.

This means:

- Letting go of baby daddy drama. No more sex with your children's fathers or anyone who is not your husband. No more allowing your children's fathers or any man to have a revolving door to your home, your resources, your vagina, or your womb. Period!

- Distance yourself from rowdy, low-vibrating friends and family members. No exceptions. Set boundaries and disassociate from them completely. No more lending money and do not borrow anything from anyone ever again. Get yourself a new tribe if you need babysitters and its best not to share any of your new plans with family.

- Eliminating any questionable or unsafe behaviors from your life. Excessive drinking should be eliminated or drastically limited. Smoking nicotine, weed, vapes or illicit drugs must stop NOW!

- Seeking therapy and beginning to do extensive work for any trauma, grief, toxic behaviors, damaging thoughts, daddy issues, depression and shame. Watch positive videos and read more books with content like this one that supports your healing and growth.

- Hit the gym if you need to drop weight and/or stay healthy. Find a hobby you enjoy and pour into yourself and your children's growth.

BONUS: Ensure your children are well behaved, loved, smart and grateful. You are responsible for your life right now so piece it back together. You can do it sis! You have a world of support out here and we are rooting for you. Your perfect mate is seeking you, so be ready!

You are a diamond in the rough, but it's time to start polishing yourself up, love. Clean up your act and prepare for the man who is worthy of you—the man who will honor and cherish **YOU** for who **YOU** are, **NOT** who **YOU WERE**.

Celebrating the Behaviors of Good Men

In a relationship landscape often marred by exploitation and superficiality, recognizing and appreciating the behaviors of good men is crucial. Good men exist, and they show their love through actions that honor and uplift their partners.

What Defines A Good Man?

A good man understands the value of treating his partner like royalty—not just through grand gestures, but through everyday actions that demonstrate respect and care. He knows that opening doors, assisting with a coat, or pulling out a chair isn't old-fashioned; it's a sign of respect. His transparency and honesty are pillars that support the foundation of your relationship, ensuring that trust is never a concern.

Good men are partners in every sense. They are genuinely interested in your goals and dreams and will pour into your aspirations without a second thought. They are not just cheerleaders, but active participants in helping you achieve your ambitions. Financial provision isn't about control, but about creating a shared space of security and comfort, allowing you to rest in your femininity and embrace your role in the relationship without undue stress.

Appreciating and Nurturing Your Relationship with A Good Man

To nurture a relationship with a good man, recognize and appreciate these qualities. Show gratitude for his efforts, and be open about your needs and desires. A relationship is a two-way street; mutual respect and appreciation go a long way in deepening your bond.

Celebrating and Encouraging Gentlemanly Conduct

Encourage and celebrate the gentlemanly conduct of your partner when you see it. Whether it's his way of respectfully disagreeing or supporting you in front of others, these behaviors are signs of a man who respects and values you deeply. They are worth more than any material offering because they come from a place of love and genuine affection.

In fostering these qualities and recognizing them in your partner, you also set a standard for how you want to be treated and show the world the type of relationships that should be aspired to.

A good man will never make you question your worth or ask you to prove your value. He will know your worth from the moment he meets you and will continue to celebrate it every day.

Warning Signs to Watch For

Ladies as you navigate your journey toward preserving your sexual energy, it's essential to stay alert to the warning signs that can derail your intentions. One significant factor is the unrealistic portrayals of love and intimacy in celebrity culture; these images often glamorize casual sex and undermine the value of waiting for a meaningful connection. Additionally, the influence of friends who may pressure you to conform to their choices can be overwhelming, especially if their relationships lack depth or commitment. Toxic music with themes that promote objectification or casual hookups can also seep into your mindset, normalizing behaviors that don't align with your values. Furthermore, reflecting on your upbringing is crucial; if you were raised in an environment that devalues self-worth or promotes unhealthy relationships, these patterns may linger in your decision-making. By recognizing these influences, you empower yourself to resist temptation and honor your commitment to preserving your Sweet 'P.'

Beware of those who diminish your worth by questioning, *"What do you bring to the table?"* This question can often be a red flag, indicating a transactional view of relationships rather than one based on mutual respect and love.

If a man is more interested in what you can provide materially or otherwise, instead of who you are as a person, it may be time to reconsider the relationship's value. Such a mindset reveals a concerning lack of depth and understanding of partnership, akin to someone looking to take rather than give—run from this mindset!

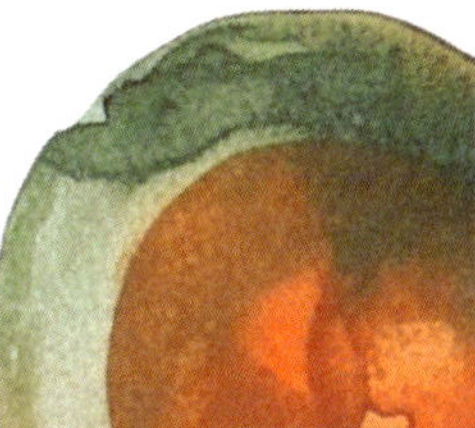

As you navigate the dating world, it's crucial to stay vigilant and recognize the red flags that signal toxic or manipulative behavior. Reading this guide will help you repel no good, toxic men, allowing you to focus on those who truly deserve your attention.

8OME RED FLAGS

Overwhelming*Charm*

While *charm* can be a delightful trait, beware when it feels overwhelming or too good to be true. Narcissists and manipulators often use charm to dazzle and disarm you, making it easier to push boundaries once they have your trust.

Rapid*Commitment*

Be cautious of someone who pushes for a commitment unusually quickly. Predators often try to lock down their targets by creating a false sense of security and intimacy, rushing commitments to bind you to them before their true colors are revealed.

Isolation*Tactics*

A significant red flag is when someone attempts to isolate you from friends, family, or any support system. They may frame it as 'us against the world,' but in reality, it's a strategy to gain control and reduce your ability to seek help or a second opinion.

How to *Gracefully* Decline and Move On

If you encounter these behaviors, knowing how to gracefully decline and move on is vital. Remain polite yet firm when expressing your disinterest. You don't need to provide lengthy explanations; a simple "I don't think we're a good match" suffices. Trust your instincts—if something feels off, it likely is.

In Case You Get Emotionally Invested

Even the best of us can get caught up. If you find yourself emotionally invested in someone who exhibits these red flags, refer back to this guide. Remind yourself of the importance of preserving your sexual energy and sticking to your boundaries. Reaffirm your commitment to waiting for the good man who will not only love and respect you but will also ask for your hand in marriage.

Embrace Your Worth: Do Not Settle for the 'Sex' of It

This book is your shield and guide. By following its lead, you prepare yourself to meet someone who is truly worthy of your time and affection—someone who sees and respects your value, not just someone who is momentarily attracted to your allure. Remember, you deserve a partner who will cherish you for more than just physical intimacy.

**You deserve a partner
who will *honor* your whole being.**

Mastering Emotional Intelligence: The Key to Preserving Your Sexual Energy

In the *journey* to preserve your body and protect your sexual energy, mastering emotional intelligence is crucial. Emotional intelligence involves not only managing your own emotions, but also recognizing and effectively responding to the emotions and intentions of others—especially those who may not have your best interests at heart.

Recognizing Manipulation

Be wary of those who use manipulation to sway you from your boundaries. Manipulators often use flattering but hollow language to achieve their own ends.

Here are some common manipulative tactics to watch out for:

Flaunting Wealth
Claims of having a lot of money or promises of lavish gifts can be used to impress and coerce.

False Uniqueness
Declarations like "I've never felt this way about anyone before" or "You are the only one who understands me" are designed to make you feel special in an insincere way.

Premature Commitment
Proclamations that "You are the one" or pushing for serious commitment early on can be red flags of a manipulative personality.

The *Art* of Being *Unbothered*

Mastering the art of being unbothered means not letting manipulative tactics affect you emotionally or sway your decisions. It involves:

Questioning Motives

Always consider why someone might be telling you what they are telling you. Are their words backed by consistent actions?

Trusting Actions Over Words

A confident, integrity-filled man will show his worth through his actions rather than merely sweet talk. He doesn't need to swindle or beguile because his intentions are honest and transparent.

Valuing Your Worth

Know that you are deserving of time, effort, honesty, and patience. Anyone not willing to invest these into your relationship is not worth your time.

Using Emotional Intelligence for Safety:
Learning to Navigate

Emotional intelligence helps you navigate interactions and relationships safely. It enables you to discern sincerity in others and identify when someone's actions do not align with their words.

If a potential suitor does not actively invest in you—as shown by their consistent actions—you remain unaffected and ready to walk away. This empowerment comes from a deep understanding of your self-worth and the unshakeable belief that you should never settle for less than you deserve.

By honing your emotional intelligence, you equip yourself with the tools needed to protect your energy and make choices that truly benefit and reflect your values. In this way, you not only safeguard your heart and body but also build a foundation for healthier, more fulfilling relationships.

How to Regulate Your Emotions

Never allow yourself to become physically angry, belligerent, or resort to profanity in response to someone else's words or actions, no matter how provoking they may be. Your true power lies in your silence and your ability to walk away. Engaging in behaviors like searching through phones, obsessively questioning your instincts, or turning into an amateur private investigator only serve to lower your vibrations and drain your emotional energy. Instead, choose to let it go. Your good man is out there searching for you, and you need to be ready—not distracted by nonsense. Maintain your focus, become unbothered by minor disturbances, and remember to never settle. By doing so, you keep yourself open to recognizing and receiving the true blessings that await you.

Stay motivated and never stop pursuing your dreams!

Men are naturally drawn to the grace and strength of positive femininity. By using this guide, you'll learn how to become more emotionally balanced and polished, creating space for healthy, positive masculinity to enter your life. When you exude femininity from within, it radiates effortlessly. This isn't about the clothes you wear, but about nurturing your inner being. Walk in your femininity for yourself, and others will notice. True femininity attracts respect and admiration—it's a quiet power that speaks volumes without ever needing to shout.

You are beautiful...
inside & out .

Building Emotional Intimacy Without Physical Expense

True emotional intimacy is built on trust, respect, and understanding. It's about connecting with someone on a deeper level, where you feel safe to be vulnerable, share your dreams, and reveal your fears. This kind of connection doesn't require physical intimacy to thrive—I am convinced, abstaining from sex can actually strengthen your emotional bond. By focusing on building emotional intimacy first, you create a strong foundation that can withstand the pressures and challenges of a long-term relationship.

If you're new to dating or re-entering the dating scene, it's essential to be upfront about your expectations and boundaries. Don't be afraid to assert yourself—good men respect a woman who knows her worth and sets clear boundaries. Low-functioning men may run at the first sign of your standards, and that's okay because you don't want them in your life anyway.

To empower yourself from the outset, focus your interactions and conversations on positive, light topics. Avoid discussions that are sexually driven, as these can derail the process of building true emotional intimacy. Instead, ask meaningful questions that reveal the character and intentions of the person you're dating.

For example, ask questions like:

- What do you see as the roles of a man and a woman in a relationship?

- How do you feel about celibacy until marriage?

- What does commitment mean to you?

- What are your long-term goals, and how do you plan to achieve them?

- What are your pet peeves?

- What are your deal breakers

Having these conversations early on allows you to filter out those who are not aligned with your values and intentions. This approach weeds out predators, players, jerks, manipulators, and time thieves, leaving you with only serious suitors who are genuinely interested in a meaningful, long-term relationship.

Self-Love Checklist

- ✔ **Wake up early**
- ✔ **Eat healthy**
- ✔ **Love**
- ✔ **Meditate**
- ✔ **Laugh**
- ✔ **Yoga & Exercise**
- ✔ **Mindfulness**

Strengthening Self-Love

Let's go a little deeper. While preserving your body for the mate who will wait is important, it's even more crucial to protect your emotional energy to avoid forming unhealthy soul ties. Think about how you feel when you meet someone and quickly feed that instant attraction with sex. Whether it happens on the first night, the second, the third, or even three months later—how do you truly feel afterward?

It's time to ask yourself some reflective questions:

- What thoughts are starting to form in your mind?
- Are you feeling anxious or frustrated?
- Are you questioning your decision?
- Do you wish you would have waited?
- Is the relationship only exciting and engaging when you're sexually active?

If your answers to these questions bring up doubts or regrets, it's a sign that something is amiss. Doubt and regret are indicators that the connection may not be as fulfilling as you hoped. Today, take a deep breath and choose to do better. Make a commitment to yourself to close shop and simply refuse to engage sexually anymore.

Have an assertive conversation with your partner that expresses your needs for a deeper emotional connection, and don't fear the outcome.

The right person will respect your boundaries and honor your journey toward self-love and emotional growth. Give yourself grace. Re-read or take time to read *Love Myself: A Roadmap for Women* and begin to strengthen your self-compassion. You deserve to nurture your emotional well-being, and by doing so, you pave the way for a love that's built on a foundation of mutual respect, trust, and true emotional connection.

Keep going, love—you're on your way to elegance, strength, and higher greatness. This journey is about more than just attracting the right mate; it's about becoming the best version of yourself. By preserving your emotional energy and sharpening your emotional intelligence, you're preparing for a relationship that's not just about commitment but about deep, enduring self-love.

Ways to *Strengthen* Emotional Connections *Without Engaging* In *Casual Sex*

- **Communicate Openly:** Share your thoughts, feelings, and experiences with your partner. Be honest about your boundaries and what you're looking for in a relationship.

- **Spend Quality Time Together:** Engage in activities that allow you to connect on a deeper level, such as taking long walks, shopping or exploring new hobbies together.

- **Engage in Deep Conversations:** Spend time discussing your values, dreams, fears, and life experiences. Sharing on this level builds trust and understanding.

- **Practice Active Listening:** Show genuine interest in your partner's thoughts and feelings. Validate their emotions and respond with empathy to strengthen your bond.

- **Plan Meaningful Dates:** Choose activities that allow for quality time and connection, such as hiking, visiting museums, cooking together, or attending cultural events.

- **Express Affection Through Words:** Write letters, send thoughtful texts, or leave notes that express your appreciation and love for your partner.

- **Develop Shared Goals:** Work together on common goals, whether it's planning a future trip, starting a project, or supporting each other's personal growth.

- **Enjoy Physical Touch Without Sexual Pressure:** Cuddling, holding hands, or giving massages can foster intimacy without the need for sexual activity.

- **Create Rituals Together:** Establish daily or weekly rituals, like a morning coffee routine or a Friday movie night, to build a sense of stability and connection.

- **Support Each Other's Passions:** Encourage and participate in each other's hobbies or interests. Showing interest in what matters to your partner deepens your connection.

- **Share Laughter and Fun:** Engage in playful activities, like board games or dancing, to create joyful memories and reinforce your emotional bond.

- **Practice Patience and Understanding:** Take time to truly know each other without rushing into physical intimacy. Building a strong emotional foundation is key to a lasting relationship.

- **Discover Your Love Language:** Learn and express each others love languages and pour into your significant other as often as possible. If you are dating feel free to be kind and loving, it is okay to be your feminine self just stay true to your boundaries.

- **Practice Emotional Support:** Be there for each other during tough times. Offer a listening ear, a comforting hug, or words of encouragement when your partner needs it.

- **Express Appreciation:** Regularly show gratitude for your partner's qualities, actions, and presence in your life. This helps to build a positive, supportive environment where emotional intimacy can flourish.

After you have healed and feel prepared to date again, consider engaging in these activities. It is crucial to focus on establishing an emotional connection with yourself initially. This self-bond encourages a deep and significant relationship rooted in self-acceptance, leading to personal development and fulfillment, ultimately benefiting all your interactions.

You are the *prize*:
Yes beautiful, your *expectations* are *perfectly realistic.*

Don't fall for society's boring standards, girl! You deserve nothing but the crème de la crème, and Mr. Right is out there looking for you. Trust me, in this huge world of people, your special someone is eager to meet you, love you and marry you BEFORE sex. He'll respect your body and your decision to save it just for him. You are a gem, so never doubt it. While others may raise eyebrows at waiting for the big "I do," stand your ground and you'll thank yourself later for not settling for less!

The Cost of Deception

There are those who may use the promise of marriage as a means to an end, presenting a ring with the intention of coaxing you into a premature physical relationship. But the cost of giving in to this deception is far too high. When you compromise your values for the illusion of commitment, you risk not only your self-respect but also the very essence of what makes your bond special. The wedding night is a sacred event, a time when you both come together in the purest form of love and commitment. To allow someone to take that away under the guise of an engagement is to shortchange both yourself and your future spouse.

The *price* of *giving* in before *vows* are *spoken* is too steep, for it costs you the *honor, dignity and self-respect* that should be *preserved* until the *marriage is sealed*.

"A ring, no matter how **dazzling**, should never be a ticket to **your body** or a shortcut to **your soul**."

RAQUEL SYMONE

The Proposal:
A Promise, Not the End

In a world where engagement rings are often used as tools of persuasion, it's crucial to hold firm to your boundaries and self-respect. An engagement ring is a symbol of a promise—a promise to marry, to love, to cherish, and to honor each other. But it is just that: a promise. The true fulfillment of that promise happens at the altar, where vows are exchanged and the marriage begins. Until then, the ring is a beautiful reminder of what's to come, but it is not the final step. Ladies your end goal is the piece of paper signed by both you, your husband and the courthouse.

It's important to recognize that while a proposal is a wonderful and meaningful gesture, it is not the same as a marriage.

**A proposal shows intent,
but marriage honors that intent by making
it real and turning words into actions.**

When you wait until your wedding night, you are doing more than just following tradition—you are making a statement about your worth. You are telling the world, and your partner, that you are not to be hurried, pressured, or deceived. You are a person of deep values, of strong convictions, and you will not be swayed by anything less than a lifetime commitment.

The wedding night is not just the culmination of your love story; it's the beginning of a new chapter, one built on trust, respect, and true devotion. By waiting, you are ensuring that your union is based on a foundation of genuine commitment, not on a fleeting moment of passion or the empty promises of an engagement ring.

57

The Wedding Night: A Celebration of Commitment and Self-Respect

In our grand oyster of life, there are few moments as significant as the one when you decide to commit to a lifelong partner. The engagement ring, sparkling on your finger, is a symbol of love, devotion, and the promise of a shared future. It's a beautiful and meaningful gesture that signals a partner's intention to marry, to build a life together, and to honor you as their chosen one. But while a proposal is a powerful expression of seriousness, it is the wedding itself—the sacred vows exchanged and the marriage that follows—that truly honors this commitment.

The Power of the Wedding Night

The wedding night is not just the finale of months of planning and anticipation; it is the moment when you and your partner finally unite in every sense—physically, emotionally, and spiritually. Waiting until this night to share yourself with your spouse is not just about preserving the sanctity of the marriage bed—it's about honoring the profound commitment you've made to each other.

By choosing to wait, you are giving the greatest gift you can offer: your whole self, unshared and unspoiled, reserved entirely for the one who has chosen to be your partner for life. This is a gift that transcends the physical and enters the realm of the spiritual. It's a celebration of your love, your self-respect, and the unbreakable bond you've created through your commitment to one another.

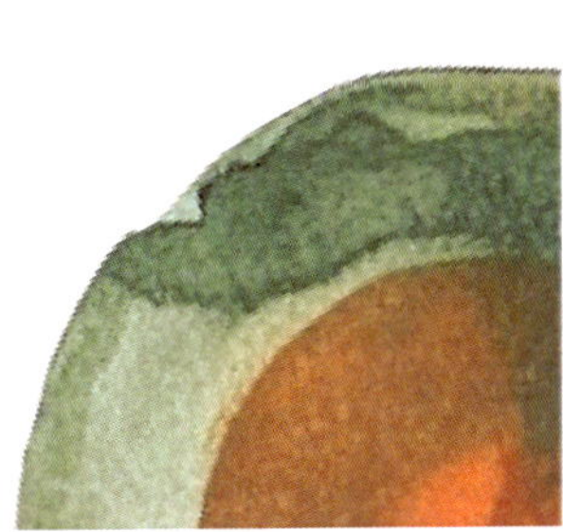

Beauty is Your Duty *Inside & Out*
Tips On Your Level Up Journey

As we journey through the process of self-love and empowerment, it's crucial to remember that loving ourselves means caring for our entire being—hair, skin, teeth, and especially our *Sweet "P"* (vagina). Embracing a holistic approach to health not only enhances our beauty, but also strengthens our physical and mental well-being.

Maintaining Your *Body's Health*

Caring for your body involves regular check-ups and being attentive to the health of your hair, skin, teeth, and vaginal wellness. Maintaining the pH balance and addressing any unusual symptoms or smells by visiting healthcare professionals can prevent common issues such as bacterial vaginosis (BV) or sexually transmitted diseases (STDs). Remember, having fewer sexual partners can significantly reduce the risk of these conditions, preserving your health and respecting your body.

Dealing with *Shame & External Pressures*

It's not uncommon to face reminders of past mistakes or pressures that advocate for an over-sexualized lifestyle. When confronted with these challenges, stand firm in your values. Surround yourself with support systems that uplift and reflect your new standards. Remember, your journey is about moving forward and growing stronger, not dwelling on the past.

Staying Clear-Headed and In Control

Eliminating or reducing alcohol and drugs from your life is essential to staying in control of your decisions, particularly when it comes to intimate relationships. Being in a clear state of mind allows you to assertively say "no" and stick to your boundaries, thus preserving your dignity and focusing on 'not settling for the sex of it.'

Always Put Forth Your Best Effort

Whether it's skin treatments that rejuvenate, dental products that enhance your smile, or gentle care for your Sweet P, find solutions that support your journey to a healthier, more confident you.

Final Thoughts

As we nurture our bodies and minds, we create a space where our true selves can thrive. This chapter isn't just about health—it's a reminder that every part of you deserves care and attention. Embrace the practice of abstinence, not just to preserve the fleeting moment of an orgasm, but to redirect that energy into building a lifetime legacy. Use this precious time to reconnect and reinvent yourself. For example, write a book, start a business, grow a garden, or learn a new language. These meaningful activities will leave a lasting impact on your life. And when your husband finds you, he'll be adding to the happiness you've already cultivated for yourself.

DISCLAIMER

SENSITIVE INFORMATION AHEAD

The next section involves topics that may provoke triggers, my apologies and empathy in advance. Embrace your strength and trust your tools of healing. If you have not sought support, you are not alone. Visit my website for more useful resources.

Trauma Bonds

Women Who Have Experienced Sexual Trauma

Dating can be a challenging experience for anyone, but for women who have experienced sexual trauma at any point in their lives it can be even more complex. The trauma you've endured may have left deep scars, making it difficult to trust, open up, or feel safe in new relationships. You may find yourself feeling hesitant, guarded, or even fearful of getting close to someone new. These feelings are valid, and your caution is both understandable and necessary for your healing journey.

Some of us may find solace in celibacy, using it as a protective measure to shield ourselves from potential hurt. If this is where you are, know that you are not wrong for creating safety. Your defenses are valid, and there is no timeline for when you should *"move on"* or *"get over it."* Healing is a deeply personal process, and you have every right to take the time you need to feel secure again. You are not obligated to rush your healing, nor should you feel pressured to do so by anyone else.

It is my hope that this book offers you support, inspiration, and a sense of empowerment. Every woman deserves to navigate the dating world with a healthy mindset, one that honors her boundaries and emotional needs. It's perfectly okay to take your time. Re-entering the world of dating after trauma can be daunting, even terrifying, but know that you are not alone in this journey.

There are indeed great men out there—men who are kind, patient, and understanding, who will respect your pace and your boundaries. The world is not filled with predators and jerks; there are men who will protect you, cherish you, and value the strength it took for you to open up again. Take comfort in knowing that you are worthy of love, care, and respect. As you move forward, be gentle with yourself, and allow yourself to heal at your own pace.

Remember, it's okay to be cautious. It's okay to move slowly. And when you feel ready, it's also okay to open your heart again. Your experiences have shaped you, but they do not define you. You have the power to create new, positive experiences, and to find the love that you deserve—one that honors your journey and your healing.

To further empower you in these early stages, remember that your boundaries are a reflection of your self-worth. Communicate them confidently and clearly, without apology. When you assert your needs and expectations, you not only protect your emotional energy but also send a strong message that you are not someone to be taken lightly.

This section isn't just about providing information—it's about giving you the tools and guidance to navigate the dating world with confidence and clarity. As you build emotional intimacy without the physical expense, you'll find that your connections are richer, more fulfilling, and more likely to lead to a relationship that honors both your body and your soul.

By prioritizing emotional intimacy, you're setting the stage for a love that's based on mutual respect, trust, and a deep understanding of one another—qualities that will stand the test of time.

Realistic Relationship Expectations Guide

Abstaining from Sex

Not everyone who tries to abstain from sex will make it until marriage. People who don't make it may experience negative feelings, such as regret.

Expectations In Marriage

Unrealistic expectations can divide couples and harm their relationship. To avoid this, couples should have open conversations about their expectations.

Respect

Respecting your future marriage before it exists can lead to a more respectful and honored marriage.

Commitment

Commitment is a conscious decision to spend your life with someone else. The wedding vows are a promise to be devoted to your partner until the end of your life.

Physical Intimacy Without Going *"All the Way"*

Physical intimacy does not mean *"going all the way"*. It is okay to express that you desire your lover. It is even healthy to kiss, hold each other close, flirt, be close and show affection with appropriate and consensual touch. Allowing yourself to be vulnerable with your mate leads to meaningful connection that leads to healthy longterm marriages and partnerships.

Saying NO is a complete sentence not a death sentence.
Be brave, be bold and be your best self for your mate.

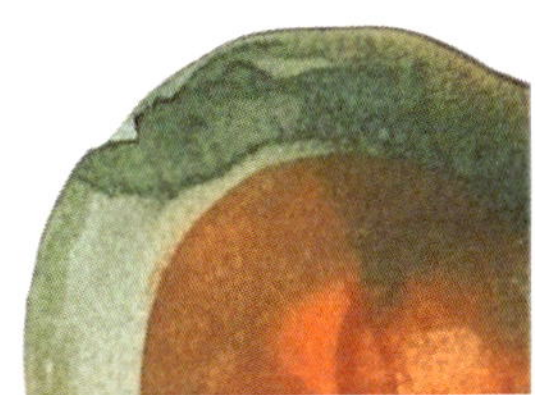

Tips for Dating As A Woman Who Has Experienced Sexual Trauma

When to Start Dating

It's essential to take your time before diving into the dating scene. Ensure you've done the necessary healing work and that you're emotionally ready to start a new relationship. There's no rush—wait until you feel strong, confident, and in control of your emotions before putting yourself out there.

Expressing Boundaries

Your boundaries are a crucial part of your healing process and should be respected by anyone you choose to date. Be clear and assertive about what you are and aren't comfortable with. A partner who genuinely cares about you will honor your boundaries and work with you to create a safe and supportive environment.

Dating for Commitment

If you're looking for a committed relationship, be upfront about your intentions from the start. Don't be afraid to express that you're not interested in casual flings or superficial connections. By setting clear expectations, you can weed out those who aren't serious about commitment and save your time and energy for someone who is.

Trusting Again

Trust is something that must be earned, especially after experiencing trauma. Take things slowly, and don't feel pressured to rush into anything. Allow your partner to prove themselves trustworthy through consistent actions and respect for your boundaries.

Self-Care and Support

Dating after sexual trauma can be emotionally draining, so it's essential to prioritize self-care. Surround yourself with a supportive network of friends, family, or community members who understand what you're going through. Consider seeking professional help from a therapist who specializes in trauma if you need additional support.

"No" is a complete sentence and a stand alone boundary. After absorbing the wisdom and therapeutic tools provided in this book, you'll find the strength and confidence to assert your boundaries without hesitation. The men you encounter after embracing this journey will respect your wishes, and you'll feel safe knowing that your *"No"* is both powerful and respected. Trust that you have the right to protect your emotional and physical well-being, and remember, you owe no further explanation, *"No"* is enough.

This guide has offered you a wealth of insight, and you may be feeling a bit overwhelmed—that's okay. Remember, you are the most important part of this journey, and your healing is the primary focus. Seeking help from a licensed professional is a crucial step toward healing. As a Veteran myself, I wholeheartedly advocate the support provided by the V.A. If you're a Veteran, I encourage you to explore the multitude of resources available to you, from counseling to health services. Additionally, consider seeking whole health coaching or entering rehab to work through any addictions. Do whatever is necessary to reclaim your well-being. You deserve the time and space to heal before engaging in or re-entering any relationships. Repair the one you have with yourself first. And remember—no more settling for the *'sex'* of it. When we know better, we do better. Now is your time to honor yourself, reclaim your power, and step confidently into your future.

NOTES

Take a moment to reflect on what you have read thus far. Write out whatever comes to mind. Put pen to paper and just write whatever feelings you are experiencing.

____

____

____

____

____

____

____

____

____

____

____

____

____

____

____

____

____

____

____

Don't Settle for the Sex of It...
and Don't Settle for the 'Social Media Effect' Either

With constant pressure to keep up with the picture-perfect lives we see on social media and the never-ending push to consume more, it's easy to lose sight of what truly matters. But self-love isn't about chasing superficial ideals or filling voids with temporary fixes. It's about doing the deep work—building your emotional intelligence, preserving your sexual energy, and growing your financial wisdom. Being your best self doesn't require an endless budget; in fact, it's priceless. Here are some ways to stay grounded as you prepare for your feminine best:

1. Prioritize Mental Health

Seek therapy, attend free support groups, and, if you're a veteran, take advantage of the free mental health and wellness services available through the V.A. Don't get caught up in the quick-fix commercials you see in 60-second TikTok videos or endless Instagram posts. Real self-care is deeper and often doesn't cost a thing—it's about positive connection to people, nature, and your inner self.

2. Practice Daily Gratitude

Be thankful for what you already have, rather than constantly seeking more. Your health, time, and skills are your greatest assets. Self-love can look like meal prepping for a healthier week or reorganizing your space and donating what you no longer need. Don't fall into the trap of overconsuming products that promise to make life easier—real self-sufficiency comes from appreciating your abilities and making your life easier with what you already have. Gratitude isn't about buying more; it's about recognizing the abundance in your current life.

3. Celebrate Your Sexual Energy

Celibacy is not a deprivation—it's a celebration of your body and soul. Embrace this time to honor your energy in ways that bring you joy, like taking a waist bead or belly dancing class. Your energy is sacred, and choosing to reserve it for those who truly value and respect you is empowering. This is a time to connect with your body on a deeper level and enjoy the beauty of nurturing your spirit without feeling the need to give it away.

4. Live Within Your Means

Financial intelligence starts with managing what you have. Stop comparing your life to others online—your wealth is in the choices you make, not in what you accumulate.

5. Nourish Your Body & Mind

Your well-being is your top priority, and it doesn't have to cost a thing. Start a garden to grow your own food, fast for spiritual clarity and cleansing, or create playlists filled with uplifting music—especially around the holidays. These simple, free activities can help you feel more connected to yourself and the world around you. Nourishment comes in many forms, and feeding both your body and your soul will make you feel stronger and more balanced.

6. Surround Yourself with Authentic People

Real relationships, not filtered snapshots, are what sustain us. Focus on building your legacy by connecting with people who can teach you something new—whether it's real estate investors or experts in a field you've always wanted to explore. Platforms like Meetup.com are a great place to start.

And remember, I, as an author, am your first connection. Start writing that book you've always dreamed of! Surround yourself with those who uplift and inspire you to be the best version of yourself.

7. Unplug and Reconnect

Limit your social media time. Instead, focus on real-life connections and experiences that nurture your growth.

Remember, no more comparing yourself to the unrealistic images you see on TV or online. The internet thrives on emotional spending, pushing products that promise fulfillment but leave you empty. Don't fall for it—you are far too savvy to settle for less than what you truly deserve. Overconsumption—whether in products or meaningless relationships—will leave you just as hollow as a fleeting encounter with someone who doesn't value you. Real beauty, real success, and real self-love come from within.

The next page is a letter I wrote to my future love. Read it and then use the proceeding page to write a letter to your future husband. *Be specific, honest, and let your heart guide you* as you envision the love you deserve. You can also use this space to not only reflect on your journey, but also write a list of qualities you want in your ideal mate. Be clear and focus on what truly matters, like kindness, loyalty, or shared values. For example, "I want someone who supports my dreams and makes me feel safe."

To My Love.

Just a moment ago, *I thought about you*, and my heart nearly skipped a beat. Before another moment passes, I want you to know how much I love you. I love you for the late-night laughs and the early morning kisses. I love you for holding my hand through the thick and thin, for keeping butterflies in my stomach, and for being a gracious human being. Most of all, I love you for being my provider, protector, lover, and the one who fills my life with endless comfort. I'm grateful for the way you honor my heart, and I cherish the love we've built on respect, kindness, devotion and unwavering support.

Raquel

Dear Future Husband,

CONCLUSION

Embrace Your Worth

Choosing to save yourself for the right man isn't about adhering to old-fashioned values—it's about recognizing your worth and refusing to settle for less than you deserve. Your body and emotional energy are precious gifts, and they should be shared only with someone who truly values and cherishes you.

Don't be ashamed of having high standards, and don't let anyone pressure you into giving away your power. Waiting for the man who will honor, respect, and choose you as his wife is a courageous and empowering decision. You're not just saving your body—you're saving your heart, your spirit, and your self-respect.

In a world that often equates sex with self-worth, choosing to wait is a radical act of self-love. You're saying to the world, "I am worthy of love, respect, and commitment. I will not settle for anything less." And in doing so, you're paving the way for a future filled with deep, meaningful connections and a love that truly lasts.

QUESTIONS?

Visit **www.raquelsymone.com** to purchase more books, merchandise, and to book Raquel Symone for speaking engagements. Explore her first book, *Love Myself: A Roadmap for Women*, and join the movement of self-love and self-respect. While you're there, you can also access exclusive resources, read her latest blog posts, and stay updated on upcoming events and workshops. Everything you need to continue your journey of *self-worth* and *empowerment* is just a click away!